HAL•LEONARD
INSTRUMENTAL
PLAY-ALONG

AUDIO
ACCESS
INCLUDED

PLAYBACK+
Speed • Pitch • Balance • Loop

TROMBONE
CHRISTMAS *Favorites*

T0088339

Audio arrangements by Peter Deneff

To access audio visit:
www.halleonard.com/mylibrary
Enter Code
1555-9045-1046-6739

ISBN 978-1-4950-9639-6

HAL•LEONARD®
7777 W. BLUEMOUND RD. P.O. BOX 13819 MILWAUKEE, WI 53213

In Australia Contact:
Hal Leonard Australia Pty. Ltd.
4 Lentara Court
Cheltenham, Victoria, 3192 Australia
Email: ausadmin@halleonard.com.au

Copyright © 2017 by HAL LEONARD LLC
International Copyright Secured   All Rights Reserved

Visit Hal Leonard Online at
www.halleonard.com

BLUE CHRISTMAS

TROMBONE

Words and Music by BILLY HAYES
and JAY JOHNSON

THE CHRISTMAS SONG
(Chestnuts Roasting on an Open Fire)

TROMBONE

Music and Lyric by MEL TORMÉ
and ROBERT WELLS

CHRISTMAS TIME IS HERE

from A CHARLIE BROWN CHRISTMAS

Words by LEE MENDELSON
Music by VINCE GUARALDI

TROMBONE

FELIZ NAVIDAD

TROMBONE

Music and Lyrics by
JOSÉ FELICIANO

HAPPY XMAS
(War Is Over)

TROMBONE

Written by JOHN LENNON
and YOKO ONO

HAVE YOURSELF A MERRY LITTLE CHRISTMAS

from MEET ME IN ST. LOUIS

TROMBONE

Words and Music by HUGH MARTIN
and RALPH BLANE

HERE COMES SANTA CLAUS
(Right Down Santa Claus Lane)

TROMBONE

Words and Music by GENE AUTRY
and OAKLEY HALDEMAN

(There's No Place Like)
HOME FOR THE HOLIDAYS

TROMBONE

Words and Music by AL STILLMAN
and ROBERT ALLEN

IT'S BEGINNING TO LOOK LIKE CHRISTMAS

TROMBONE

By MEREDITH WILLSON

MELE KALIKIMAKA

TROMBONE

Words and Music by
R. ALEX ANDERSON

MERRY CHRISTMAS, DARLING

TROMBONE

Words and Music by RICHARD CARPENTER
and FRANK POOLER

ROCKIN' AROUND THE CHRISTMAS TREE

TROMBONE

Music and Lyrics by
JOHNNY MARKS

RUDOLPH THE RED-NOSED REINDEER

TROMBONE

Music and Lyrics by
JOHNNY MARKS

SILVER AND GOLD

TROMBONE

Music and Lyrics by
JOHNNY MARKS